www.finishinglinepress.com

What I Can Carry

poems by

Laurie Elizabeth Lambert

Finishing Line Press
Georgetown, Kentucky

What I Can Carry

This collection is for my Mom and Dad,
Evelyn and Leonard Lambert.

ACKNOWLEDGMENTS

I am grateful for the support and encouragement of fellow writers at Women
Writing for (a) Change. I'm indebted to Chris, Claire, Hannah, Owen and
Mary K for their generosity, patience and inspiration.

Publisher: Leah Maines

Editor: Christen Kincaid

Cover Art: Owen Kelling

Author Photo: Hannah Kelling

Cover Design: Elizabeth Maines

Printed in the USA on acid-free paper.
Order online: www.finishinglinepress.com
          also available on amazon.com

Author inquiries and mail orders:
Finishing Line Press
P. O. Box 1626
Georgetown, Kentucky 40324
U. S. A.

Table of Contents

My Advice

To check for a fever,
don't feel the forehead,
instead
kiss your child's neck.
Let your lips linger til you're sure.
It's hot.
It's not hot.
Your lips will tell you.

Here is why:
The neck is a cozy sheltered corner
rich in circulation,
it never misrepresents
as does the brow, exposed,
sweaty with effort
or buffeted by breezes.
And
your lips are so very sensitive
to touch
and to temperature,
more perceptive than
your tired palm.

Here is another why:
How sweet, how intimate,
how immeasurably tender
to express your concern,
your curiosity, and your caring,
with a gentle, unhurried, inquiring kiss.
And
if you are lucky like me, one day
when your child, now much taller,
and looking less than well,
sits down and asks you
to check his neck,
you will find
your grateful lips lingering
on a soft, tender, bristly spot.

Mine

I used to have stuff that was mine
scarves and shoes, jewelry and knick knacks
pens, water bottles, flashlights
mirrors and combs and brushes
a special vase
a favorite coffee mug
a soft sweater from my best friend

Sometimes I find these things broken
soggy, torn, discarded, or crumpled
some lost treasures bring tears to my eyes
some things I probably never miss

I have surrendered my stuff
both the unique and the mundane

Bartered

For stained cloth, broken glass, single earrings
and more

For a taste of your lumpy red licorice milkshake
the sticky brownie you saved for me from the party

For the red leaf you gave me that was shaped like a heart
the stone that you found by the river and put in my pocket

For the heron feather that you tucked into my braid
the handful of sand you brought me from the beach

For your whispered
"I love you Mom"

Adolescent Blues

a flash of red caught my eye
just outside my bathroom window
and stopped me
in the midst of my ablutions

a strange looking bird
sitting on a branch
a dull whitish chest and
just those few red feathers

I tried to place elements
of his shape, his size
the style of his head
and then he turned and
oh my god
the blue
just there
a streak of blue

my nose close to the
window, I peered at him
glad he was in no hurry
nondescript brown, gray, white
splotching, stripey,
checkish on the wings,
but with a telling shape
to the brow and beak
and that splash of red
on the white breast
that unmistakable blue
at the edge of the wing

my palm to my forehead
ah yes, it must be, surely
a teenaged bluebird

thank you my sweet
for this long long look at you this morning
what a silly-looking thing you are
mostly ordinary, drab, unremarkable
but with those bits of bold color
foretelling your future
what a chance you have given me
to see the becoming

Barometer

I love it when my girl
sings in the shower
I sit on the couch
and listen to her soprano
reaching, soaring, silky

surely a throat cannot make
that kind of sound
without at least contentment
if not bliss
in the heart that beats beneath it

Tempest

walking a narrow path beside the cornfield
deep in shadow between the woods' edge
and the towering maize, the stirring begins
movement, noise, like a wind
rustling the leaves on the soaring stalks

black birds, first a pair
flying from the corn to the trees
then a dozen follow
and in the next instant
a dark and thunderous storm of feathers
as hundreds move together
across and above this narrow space
in the midst of this murmuration
I can almost touch the black wave

Triage

There's a busted pipe under my sink.
It's not the one where the water comes In
that means I have to search the basement
and find where to turn off the water.
No
it's the one where the water goes Out
out the drain from the sink
the one that means
NO!
do NOT wash your hands
before you begin to take out
allllll the stuff you keep
under the sink.
Get the bucket
(first).

Anything in powder form is history.
Heavy, sogged, but just wet.
Exploring further, the true implications
of the term "gray water"
are clarified.
All the times we've rinsed and rinsed those things
poked and prodded those things
to get them to go, yes
GO
down the drain.
Here they are! HelloHello!

Determined grains of rice clinging
to the spray can of furniture polish.
Little erts of broccoli sprinkled
on the rubber gloves.
Crunchy shards scraped from frying pan
sprayed on the rubber mat.
Specks of scrambled egg
dribbled on the dish strainer.
That delicious mixture
of mashed potatoes and bacon
now schmeared greasily
into the bag
of sponges.

Lupa Capitolina

There's no halfway with the SheWolf
When it's on, it's all the way on.
It's a toggle switch, not a dial.

My daughter was in the hospital for outpatient
knee surgery. Prep Nurse said
"We've had an absolutely terrible day for iv's.
Can't hit a vein for anything!"
Then she sat on the edge of the bed
and asked my girl to hold out her arm

SheWolf took over then, golden eyes
on my girl's arm and the nurse's gloved hands.
With the sheer power of my presence I
guided the needle smoothly into place.

Prep Nurse attached tape, intravenous tube, and stood up
saying cheerfully "Well, that went smoothly!
Maybe we've turned the corner." My girl let out
a long deep breath and her face relaxed.
Then Anesthesiologist arrived, and they told me
to leave the room and wait down the hall while
he administered a Nerve Block.

They should have let me stay and help again.
It took a double dose of sedative to settle my girl,
and when I got back to her she was
loopy, gone, stepped out.

Soon Surgeon came in to check on her. She did not
recognize him, but with a deeply furrowed brow
and all kinds of effortfull concentration she was able
to say "right knee" when prodded, verbally and physically,
to state the purpose of her presence.
They shoo'ed me out then, to The Waiting Area
and took her to The Surgery Suite.
I waited. I read, I knitted, I drank tea,
I ignored the droning television.

I held in a whine, I tried to keep my anxiety penned.

It was a hell of a long wait, like at a restaurant
when people who came in after you get seated
before you, and then it happens again.
Finally Desk Lady called my girl's name.
I bolted from my seat, and she took me to
a room across the hall to wait for Surgeon.

I waited. I tried not to look at the clock. I opened
my book but couldn't read the words.
I stood and paced the length of the table
tail twitching, consumed by the waitingness
of these minutes ticking.

Surgeon arrived after half an hour or so. He said things went smoothly
and gave me details about what he had done inside my girl's knee.
He told me it would be about an hour before
I would be called back to see her. He shook my hand,
nodded to my Thank You, left. I went back to The Waiting Area.

The hour mark passed and then more. Desk Lady packed up
her stuff and said goodbye. She told the few remainders,
as she put a phone on the countertop, that we should pick up
if it rang, and hand it to the family of whosever's name was said.
A while later, it rang and someone closer picked up. Not I.
Another while, another ring, again not for me.

The third time at the first vibration She Wolf
loped across the room and picked up before
the first ring had died. And yes,
it was my girl's name they said, and I
went wagging through the double doors
to that land called Recovery.

I found my girl, put my hand on her hand on the sheet.
Her eyes were closed and she did not respond to my touch
with even a flutter of an eyelid. Recovery Nurse
came to me at the bedside. She asked if I had heard my girl
earlier. I said "what?" She said "she was screaming
when she woke up. There were some pain control problems.
She was out of control thrashing and…"

I could feel my incisors lengthening,
a growl rumbled in my throat, "No," I said
"I didn't hear her." She Wolf would have been in here
tearing things apart if I had heard my girl
screaming in pain.

They had given her another Nerve Block to stop the pain,
the screaming. That screaming that happened
that I didn't hear then.

I could hear its echo now.

For a minute, I think Recovery Nurse considered
sending me back to The Waiting Area until
my girl woke up. I could see these thoughts,
and then their rejection, in her eyes.
I stayed leaning on the bedrail, hackles up,
holding my girl's hand and watching her face
for any sign of discomfort, or of waking.
There was no where, no one, else for me.

My girl roused after a while, I wasn't counting time
anymore. She was frightened, shook, but not in pain.
We moved quickly to get her headed elsewhere.
The bed rolled to the Outward Bound Department.
Exit Nurse measured some things,

pulled out the iv and found some scrubs that would fit
over the giant bandaged and braced leg.
She put my girl in a wheelchair, told me to pull my car up
to the exit, and started rolling toward the hall

I had the car warm by the time they approached.
We tried the front, but I saw my girl wince
when Exit Nurse moved to close the door, and
the hairs on the back of my neck stiffened.
Nurse let go of the door, and we gingerly returned
my girl to the wheelchair and then put her in the back
sitting sidewise with that poor leg lying on the seat.

We waved goodbye and drove away,
my girl and me, on the long road,

back to the den.

The River

On a day like today
this river is my friend
On a day like today perhaps also
my salvation

Today the river felt like a good book
that I will never come to the last page of
Always there always open
always telling a good part
of the story it has to tell
Never the same words twice

Over the years the river and I
have shared our tales with each other
and we each have aged
and changed our courses

We've weathered by turns raging floods
and periods of rainlessness
that both test the meaning of the word 'river'

I have stood at the edge
of the rushing pushing boundless bankless mass
carrying things broken and abandoned
and the river has borne my fury and fear

I have walked the track of dry rocks
felt the absence the want of water
smelled the fish stranded in disconnected puddles
and shared my own hunger and grief

But today the river was a fairy tale
page after page of joyful syllables
babbling of lovers reunited
chortling babies
chiming carillons

and I was dancing

Pie

There's a pecan pie my Mom made
in my freezer hidden deep.
The next time she visits me
she'll make me another
and after she has gone home
I'll freeze the fresh one
and eat the one that's waiting frozen now.

She doesn't know about this practice,
the successive secreting of pies.

I live in Ohio,
my Mom lives in Massachusetts and
she's 83 years old.
My Mom spends 48 weeks
of every year at home
and 4 weeks of every year
with me.

I can do the math.
Chances are
the day she slips these earthly bonds
we will not be together
and may not have seen each other
for a couple of whiles.

Each time she visits
she brings me something
a picture, a letter, a candy dish
a scarf, a pin, coins.
She brings a bit of history with each of them,
often stories of their gifting,
from whom, when.
It's the stories, more than the pieces,
that are treasures.

Perhaps she believes
these objects will comfort me,
or perhaps it comforts her
for me to have them.

This is what comforts me:
the sight of her covered with flour
and my kitchen table and floor snowed upon.
The purposefulness of her stroke with the rolling pin,
her smile when the pecans float to the top.
The decisiveness of her proclamations
"done!" or "needs another five."

This is what comforts me:
to have a Plan.

When she's gone,
gone from here and from there
I am going to get a phone call.
I'm going to buy a plane ticket.
I'm going to make sure
there are no gladiolas at her wake
and I'm going to sing and
cry loudly at her funeral.

When I come back home to Ohio
knowing she will not come again
I'm going to drink a Presbyterian
with three cherries with stems.
The same highball I made for her
every evening of every visit.

I may spend some time with
those belongings
she has brought me,
remembering the stories.

But what I think
I will really need
if I can bear it,
to hold it in my mouth,
is the sweetness,
the love
in that pie.

Shake me up
(after Shake my Future by Dorothea Smartt)

Shake my future
Take the snow globe of my life
and turn it upside down
Feed my spirit, give me what I need
to step out, step forward
to shape a day, a month
a year of promises kept

Shake my future
Poke a hole in the bubble of fear
caught in my throat
keeping me from taking a deep breath
and speaking my mind
Move me toward greater boldness
confidence
strength

Shake my future
Push me forward in giant strides
not the hesitating baby steps
that trap me, complacent, in the present

Shake my future
Let my preconceived notions and misconceptions
be damned and dismantled
Open me up to fresh style of seeing and feeling
Bring me to a new way of being in the world

Shake my future
Shake me up
Break me into pieces
and watch me put myself back together
into someone newly born and beautiful

Labyrinth

We had walked this way once before and
 I remember remarking with some wonder
"this just takes all the hurry right out of you."
So I was surprised that my friend seemed
almost rushed. She set out before me
at what I deemed a bit of a clip, but then
the shoulders and curves of the course
brought her to a gentler pace. She slowed
and evened her steps, and I resisted the urge
to catch up to her shadow, instead
hanging back several paces and relaxing too,
in both my thoughts and my footsteps.
As we walked the convoluted passage
inside the circle, we seemed to experience
every imaginable pattern of travel-for-two.

I was behind her on the same path, or on a
parallel trail. We walked toward each other, then
in contrary courses, we turned to pass
on different tracks, always on a bending
route, turning, sometimes nodding,
sometimes passing with heads bent
in contemplation. In time we arrived
at the bench at the circle's center,
and we sat facing opposite directions,
with our shoulders and our spines
leaning heavily against each other
feeling the warmth of the backs of our bodies
against the cold of the day on our faces.
I believe if one of us had stood, the other
would have fallen over. We spoke
quietly about our trip through this circle, and
how this traverse resembled our lives and our
friendship. Coming together, moving apart,

closeness followed by distance, again and again,
and in the end, the warmth and sense of belonging
that we give to each other, the nourishment of being
with someone that holds you so very dearly.

I take myself back to that labyrinth often,
I see again that winsome smile on her face
as we strode toward each other, then
passed at our shoulders, a dance, a do-si-do.
The look of her nether and her gait as I followed her,
the peace and rhythm of our strides
when we were side by side, and salient,
the comfort of hearing her footfalls behind me,
out of sight but with me still, and ever.

Leaving

over the river they are falling
huge sycamore leaves and their smaller cousins
downward dancing

yellow, deep cranberry
even the brown ones are still supple
they do not crumble

dropping into the flow
they sink to decay underwater
giving the river smell and pigment

tumbling through the rushes
they muffle the river's music
to deep soft notes

stopped on jutting rocks and sticks
they stack like carelessly sorted mail
and the water is diverted

next Spring from these leaves
there will remain a trace of scent, paint
a new song, a shifted path

Stick Together

Fear whispered in my ear

I have heard too many stories
of teen tragedies
young lives ending
in a deranged moment of hopelessness

I have read that teenagers kill themselves
because they cannot see past today
they do not feel the future
stretching in front of them

Lost in the agony of an instant
they cannot bear to take another breath
they are finished

Because I believe this may be true
I find myself on the phone
with somebody's mom
giving voice to my own fear
in a story I cannot
Not Tell

"your son has told my daughter
he is going to end his life"

In my own heart I am begging
God, Joseph, Mary and Jesus
all the saints, sisters, and spirits
to Save Mine

Save me and mine
from this sightlessness
Give me and mine the vision
in any moment of despair
even if a heart is breaking
to See Each Other
to gasp another gulp of air
and another, and keep breathing
for each other

November Blues

out the window a bluebird sat
on the bare branch of a maple

seemed late for a bluebird
but as I watched
he was joined by another
blue here, blue there
another and another

flitting around and changing places
in a tangled blue dance
up and down from tree to bush
to lawn and tree again

a dozen, perhaps twenty
a mixture of vivid males
and drabber girls

not just the blue
their chests too were more red
their bellies a bright gleaming white
in this Novemberness
of gray clouds, dying grass
and skeleton trees

one by one they travelled
from the side yard
to the front of the house
and then down the hill
across the road

Away

Lament

my girl was crying in the shower
howling, wailing
pounding her fist on the wall
body racked with sobbing
chest heaving
face slick with tears and mucous

sounds coming out
from a place
never ever heard from before
a deep place
filled with sounds of breaking glass and
blood gurgling blackish red from a wound

helpless, useless
on the step outside the door
an echoing sound rippled
from that same place in my belly
my face hot with
her sorrow, her hurt
and an anger that was all my own

unaware until this moment
that she loved him
from that deep place
I burned to find him
shake him senseless

Ardor

It started months ago, with books.

Pictures of ancient beautiful trees
alive and bent, contorted with age
or alive and enormous
a whole world sheltered by the branches of one tree.

Detailed drawings of the veins of leaves
explaining the way leaves breathe
diagrams and equations
showing the layers of bark
the movement of water and carbon dioxide and oxygen.

Trees became more significant
and noticeable parts of the landscape.
In my walks through the woods I began to stop,
and look up, following the trunk through the branches
up to the sky, and I saw the reaching, the strength, the grace.

I read more books, about the spirituality
of the beings that we call trees
here for eons, millions of years longer
than anything remotely resembling a mammal.

Trees breathed this planet to life.

And in me grew, like a seed opening,
a need, a desire
a curiosity, a voice.

A book told me how to befriend a tree:
stand near
send a message of respect
ask permission and then
approach, touch
wait.

I visited a tree that I admired
followed the instructions from the book,
and my reverence for this tree grew
but this tree did not respond to me.

I did not give up. I did not push.
I stopped thinking about the trees so much
and started to just be among them
in a new way.

On an autumn day, I strayed from my usual walk
and went out to the woods on a ridge line
at the northmost point of my land.

I stopped at The Leaning Tree, so named
because it hangs out over the edge of the ridge
looking like it wants to take flight
in spite of its enormity.

I stood for a while near to The Leaning Tree
spoke my intention
to lay my hands on its skin of bark
and then I did so
trying not to put too much weight there.

Perhaps it was the strange tilting posture
after a moment, I felt an invitation
I leaned forward and lay entirely upon the tree
my head turned sideways,
resting on a very accommodating bump
so that my ear and cheek
were clear of the bark's rough surface
just my temple resting on that bump
and then the whole of the rest of me embracing
hoping that another 130 pounds was not too much
for The Leaning Tree.

My breathing changed
air seemed to travel farther within me
to an opening space,
a place that had not breathed before.

Yes

I lay in my bed
listening to the night noises
through the open window
I am cold
but I like these noises

I turn to my left
shape my body into
a letter "C"
tuck my fingers under
to warm them

I feel my bones
through thin cloth
the ridges of my ribs
beneath the skin

I spread my fingers
to nestle in the soft valleys
between the row of bones

I can feel the beating of my heart
th-thump   th-thump
swelling rhythmically
against the lengths of my fingers

this large heart, mine
throbbing in the dark
pushing, moving my blood
my life, around the all of me

each beat saying
yes, please
and tomorrow again
yes yes   yes

Writing Space

a black stone elephant
a mottled sculpture of a pregnant woman on her knees
a stone chalice
an incredible number of loose rocks
and quite a few feathers
a mug with no handle filled with smooth stones
a hummingbird's nest
a pair of giant purple mussel shells from the river
a finger labyrinth
a wooden pelican
a small very happy red Buddha
an aluminum loon
a green iron bell shaped like a bird
a colorful bowl holding a collection of river glass
and a cast iron plate
painted with a bright blue sky and two seagulls

several of these things are gifts
but most of what is here spoke to me
at a store, or a field, or a riverbank
or a festival of people selling things they made with their hands
each one said
"take me home, put me on your writing table, I will help you."
all these scattered objects are holding me when I sit here
these rocks and feathers and doodads are
my team
my sponsors
my supporters
it makes me feel big to sit here
not big like important
but big like powerful and full and capable
I can sit here and write something
It will be me, it must be, if it came from here

Calling

it begins with the quickening
the tickle thrum and poke
of life inside your belly

followed by the giving
of birth   when the miracle
of a new beginning
repurposes every and each
of your remaining days

soon you are teaching your child
to speak your name
not the name your mother gave you
    your love-name

you stare into that beautiful face
and say "mmmmm" "mmma"
"mmom" and hope and wait and listen
and wait and hope and want

WantWantWant
to hear your new name
from those pouty precious lips

one day   it happens
when you're not trying
or even thinking about it
you hear that first "Mama"

and something inside of you
pops   like the tiny green
beginning of a plant pops out
  of the March mud
and greets the sun
around which its life will orbit

from this day to forever
you are Mama, Mommy, Mom
hearing your name

spoken tearfully
in the middle of the night

pathetically
as ears and tummies ache

triumphantly
after that soccer goal

jubilantly when
the prom date is found

from the basement
the back yard, the bathroom
from upstairs and the front porch
for years and years and years
you are called

Mommy, Mama, Mom

when your house is empty
it's there still

   the calling

a bird noise in the yard
something on the radio
the dog's whine
or a television commercial

whispers, cries, echoes

and when your grown children
visit, you hear   those   voices
talking about the weather
or politics or food
and when they say
'from' or 'milk'
or 'pussywillow'
you find yourself
coming down the stairs
saying "did you call?"

because everything
   everything
sounds like Mom

Dissolved

I am visiting a new river today
to see if she has anything to tell me
I can hear her singing
as I approach the bank
and see the swollen brown
muddy gushing with new rain
green shoots bending in the flow
the noise and motion intoxicating
I step in, sit down and crab-walk
with my hands and feet and butt
over to the shallow rapids

I lay my self down
the whole of me, head to heels
pressing against the rocks
I close my eyes to listen
(speak to me beloved)
the music of the water on the rocks
hypnotic, the inside of my eyelids
a mosaic of green and blue
for a moment
I disappear into the river

Wake, Sing

my thinker's tinkerer's head
is looking for rest
a moment of repose
surrender

my soul does not know
the notes to its own song
the words
the rhythm

dear space within me
waiting
to be filled

with the music
of understanding

with the harmony
of a new knowing

tune your strings

clear your throat

raise your hands above the drum

What I Can Carry

It's true, indeed, that there is always a rock in my pocket.
Often more than one, and frequently one or two in my other pocket
as well. I look for clothes with deep pockets, not
those token patches, I mean the kind that start at the hip,
and end at the knees, the kind you can hide your hands in
while you are fondling the rocks in your pockets.

It's true, too, that I have taken the time on occasion
to consider why, and whether or not, and if. I've mulled
all those questions about keeping rocks in my pockets,
and in my house as well. Alongside the lamps and family photos,
on shelves, tables, and windowsills, in jars, bowls, baskets
or just plain sitting. I wonder why I so enjoy these unyielding guests,
these silent visitors that bring the outside to the inside of my home.
Many have been carried here by those living in this house,
from places we will likely never roam again. Some have been brought
to me and mine as gifts from far away whereabouts
by dear friends and family.
Still others have just wandered in from the back fields and the river,
for a richly deserved sigh of wonder and appreciation.

It's true, as well, that this morning as I fingered through
the rocks on my dresser, exploring and deciding which four
or so to hold today in the generous pockets of my jeans,
I considered once again the question of why.
The answer came as this:

A tree will not fit in my pocket, though many a tree
I've wished to take along with me on my journeys.
I cannot carry the river with me wherever I go,
though I feel its current in my blood.
Geese V'ing over the horizon, the wind,
the rain, the cloud that looked like my
Grandmother's hair, the smell of mud, birdsong,
all these I cannot even touch, and yet I hold them in
my heart with great affection and desire.

All these I leave behind me,
but I can take this rock, this piece
of the beauty that is the world
and carry it in my pocket.

Laurie Lambert was born and raised in West Springfield, Massachusetts, the middle child of three sisters. After studying chemistry at Williams College, she continued her education at the University of Wisconsin-Madison and received a PhD in Medical Microbiology and Immunology. Laurie then worked as a research scientist in the pharmaceutical industry for ten years studying inflammation, arthritis and asthma.

When Laurie's family grew from 2 to 5 in one step in 1994, she cut back to part-time scientist, and eventually left this career to become a fulltime Mom to triplets (Claire, Hannah and Owen) and a substitute teacher in their school district.

As the triplets transitioned to college, Laurie began to pursue an interest in the writing life. She attended core classes at Women Writing for (a) Change in Cincinnati and eventually attended their Conscious Feminine Leadership Academy. Currently, Laurie is a certified facilitator at Women Writing for (a) Change. Laurie has also pursued an interest in activism through the V-Day organization, whose aim is the prevention of violence toward women and girls. She and her husband, Chris, have spent the last 25 years at the family home, a 50 acre paradise in Warren County, Ohio, on Todd's Fork of the Little Miami River.

Laurie's poems have been published in *Labyrinth Pathways* (2014), *Annapurna* (2015) and *For a Better World* (2013, 2015). She is a member of the Greater Cincinnati Writer's League. This is her first collection of poetry.